THE BIGGEST GIFT

A RHYMING CHRISTMAS NATIVITY PLAY SCRIPT FOR KIDS

ADRIANNA COX

MARTIN SOMMERSBY

Copyright © 2024 Hope Books Ltd

All rights reserved.

No part of this book may be reproduced in any form or by any electronic or mechanical means, including information storage and retrieval systems, without written permission from the author, except for the use of brief quotations in a book review.

CONTENTS

Introduction — v
Cast of Characters — vii

1. Scene 1 : The Stable — 1
2. Scene 2 : The Wise Men — 7
3. Scene 3 : The Shepherds — 15
4. Scene 4 : The Manger — 21
5. Scene 5 : The Dream — 25
6. Scene 6 : The Biggest Gift — 29

INTRODUCTION

Thank you for considering "The Biggest Gift" for your Christmas Navity. This rhyming play is designed to engage children and adults alike, bringing the timeless story of Jesus' birth to life in an accessible way.

"The Biggest Gift" is based on the Bible version of the Christmas story while incorporating rhyme and humor to create a enjoyable and memorable experience.

This play is suitable for children in the age range of 7 to 12 years old, While younger children (5-6 years old) could potentially

INTRODUCTION

participate with additional support, and older children or teenagers could also perform it.

The play is written to be performed as a school Christmas play or a Sunday School Nativity. The role of Narrator could be split between multiple narrators. At the end of each scene, there is a suggested Christmas carol to be sung. Feel free to omit or choose your own!

The script is designed to be flexible, allowing for adaptation to suit your specific needs and resources. You can adjust the number of characters, add or remove lines, and incorporate your own creative elements to make the play uniquely yours.

May you have fun as you celebrate the true meaning of Christmas!

CAST OF CHARACTERS

Cast List

Narrator

Mary

Joseph

Innkeeper

King Herod

Wise Men 1

Wise Man 2

Wise Man 3

CAST OF CHARACTERS

Shepherd 1

Shepherd 2

Shepherd 3

Optional:

Child 1

Child 2

Child 3

Child 4

Child 5

Child 6

Additional Cast Members

Shepherds on the hillside

Crowd going to see the baby Jesus

Angels

Stars

ONE
SCENE 1 : THE STABLE

Narrator

More than 2000 years ago

Around this time of year,

Shone a bright star,

Telling that Jesus' birth was near.

The angel Gabriel told Mary

She would give birth to a King,

So Joseph married her

and gave her a ring.

They went to Bethlehem,

under King Herod's order,

So all could be counted

by the census recorder.

As they travelled

By the light of the moon

Mary told Joseph the

Baby was coming soon.

Joseph was worried,

He knocked on every door,

But no one had room for them,

not even on the floor.

(Joseph knocks on door, and the inn keeper opens up)

JOSEPH

Excuse me, please sir,

do you have a room to spare?

Nothing fancy, we're tired,

we'll sleep anywhere.

We've knocked on every door,

and they all said no.

We need somewhere warm

for my wife and I to go.

INN KEEPER

Bethlehem's so busy,

it's quite a sight!

ADRIANNA COX & MARTIN SOMMERSBY

I don't have a room,

not even a bite!

All I can offer is my stable

so small,

But it's warm and cozy,

with room for you all!

Narrator

They made a bed in the stable

and settled right in.

And later that night,

Jesus was born, the new King!

Narrator / Child 1 (Optional)

A town small and quiet,

Our story has begun,

Let's sing about Jesus,

God's own precious Son.

Carol (Optional) : O Little Town of Bethlehem

TWO
SCENE 2 : THE WISE MEN

(Enter the 3 wise men)

WISE MAN #1

Look! In the East,

a star shines so bright,

It tells of a king

born on this night

Wise man #3

We can't leave yet,

we have no gifts to bring,

what gifts are good for a baby

and fit for a King?

Wise man #2

I think a warm blanket

and maybe a bed.

He will need somewhere soft

to lay his sleepy head.

Wise man #1

No bed! But a blanket,

That's good for a baby.

Gifts fit for a king?

I wonder, just maybe?

You are, of course, right,

A baby King shouldn't be cold.

Let's also take some

myrrh, frankincense, and gold.

NARRATOR

They packed their bags

and put on their shoes

set off to find the

new King of the Jews.

WISE MAN #1

Do we have a road map?

Bethlehem's pretty far.

WISE MAN #2

We don't need one!

ADRIANNA COX & MARTIN SOMMERSBY

Just follow that star.

Narrator

So they got on their camels

Rode over sand dunes deep

And travelled 'til they came upon

A town fast asleep

Wise man #3

Shall we stop at the palace?

It's where kings reside.

The babe we are seeking

Must be inside.

(Enter Herod)

THE BIGGEST GIFT

King Herod heard of a new king in town,

He wasn't about to give a baby his crown!

He found three of the wisest men he knew

And told them to seek out this new baby Jew.

KING HEROD

Find baby Jesus and

report back right away.

Search every home,

don't waste a single day.

(King Herod leaves and wise men turn to talk to each other)

NARRATOR

Herod was grouchy,

but they didn't care,

They had a star-map

To help leading them there!

Over hills and through valleys,

the star was their guide,

Till they found some shepherds

on the hillside.

(Shepherds approach the wise men)

Shepherd #1

Who goes there

at this time of night?

Do you know what this star is

That's shining so bright?

WISE MAN #2

We followed the star

To find the new King,

What can you tell us,

Do you know anything?

NARRATOR / CHILD 2 (OPTIONAL)

Three kings came from far away,

Following the star so bright,

Let's sing of their journey now,

On this special night.

Carol (Optional) : We Three Kings

THREE
SCENE 3 : THE SHEPHERDS

SHEPHERD 1

While watching our flocks on a starry night,

A sudden light gave us quite a fright!

An angel appeared, shining so bright,

Telling of a king born this very night.

SHEPHERD 1

The angel spoke of peace on Earth,

And told us where to find this birth.

ADRIANNA COX & MARTIN SOMMERSBY

In Bethlehem, in a manger lay

The promised child, born this day.

Shepherd 3

Then the sky filled with angels fair,

Their voices ringing through the air.

"Glory to God," they sang on high,

"And peace to all," rang through the sky.

Narrator

The wise men walked

and the shepherds they ran

And soon people joined in

and a crowd began.

(A crowd gathers)

They made their way

through the dark streets,

Singing, dancing,

and busting some beats.

The crowd grew bigger

as they drew near.

Shepherds and wise men,

all gathered here.

WISE MAN #3

Stop, look up!

The star is so bright!

It's twinkling and shining

with all its might!

ADRIANNA COX & MARTIN SOMMERSBY

Narrator

The crowd hushed and gathered around

Had the King finally been found?

They held their breath, excited to see

What this special surprise might be

One of the wise men gave

a small knock on the door

No-one could guess just

what lay in store.

In the middle of the room,

in a small wooden manger

Lay baby Jesus,

our long-awaited Saviour.

Narrator / Child 3 (Optional)

Around the manger,

let's all sing,

Of Jesus Christ,

our newborn King!

Carol (Optional) : Away in a Manger or Hark the Herald Angels Sing

FOUR
SCENE 4 : THE MANGER

WISE MAN #1

Sorry to bother you,

may we come in?

We have quite a few

gifts to bring.

JOSEPH

Come in, come in,

on this special night,

And behold the child

who brings peace and light.

(*Three wise men and shepherds enter the stable*)

NARRATOR

The three wise men went in,

On that special day,

And gazed down at the child,

Lying in the hay.

WISE MAN #2

I told you we should have brought him a bed,

He lies in a manger where animals are fed!

But he's snug as a bug, in this hay-filled nest,

Fast asleep (and) having a rest.

MARY

Don't worry. It's fine.

He is warm and cozy,

Look at his cheeks

they are nice and rosy.

NARRATOR

There lay the child,

So peaceful and still.

Not wearing a crown,

Though one day He will.

As they presented their gifts

Not one was dry-eyed.

And each of them knelt

By the tiny child's bedside.

They worshipped the King

So small and so new,

God's promise of love

For me and for you.

Narrator / Child 4 (Optional)

Come, one and all,

let's sing with cheer,

The first Noel,

for all to hear!

Carol (Optional) : The First Noel

FIVE
SCENE 5 : THE DREAM

NARRATOR

The wise men dreamed

Of Herod's wicked plan.

They woke up worried,

And quickly they ran.

They left another way,

To keep Jesus from harm.

The babe slept peacefully,

Safe in Mary's arms.

An angel appeared

To Joseph that night:

"Take Mary and Jesus,

To Egypt take flight!"

So to Egypt they travelled

Far from harm's way,

God's plan unfolding

With each passing day.

Narrator / Child 5 (Optional)

The night is silent, all is calm,

Our troubles soon will cease

THE BIGGEST GIFT

Let's sing of this holy night,

As Jesus sleeps in peace

Carol (Optional) : Silent Night

SIX
SCENE 6 : THE BIGGEST GIFT

NARRATOR

So this is the story of how Jesus came,

Born in a manger, but a King just the same!

As we celebrate this time of year,

Remember the biggest gift is already here.

Jesus came as a gift for all,

Big and small, short and tall.

And that's the end of our play

We wish you a blessed Christmas Day.

We hope you will enjoy

this Christmas season,

But remember,

Jesus is the biggest reason!

Narrator / Child 6 (Optional)

With hearts full of wonder,

let's all sing,

And celebrate the birth

of our King!

Carol (Optional) : Joy to the World

www.ingramcontent.com/pod-product-compliance
Lightning Source LLC
Chambersburg PA
CBHW070340120526
44590CB00017B/2969